Carlo Mollino

CARLO MOLLINO
ARCHITECTURE AS AUTOBIOGRAPHY

Carlo Levi, 'Multiple portrait' drawing of Carlo Mollino, *c.* 1940

GIOVANNI **BRINO**

CARLO MOLLINO
ARCHITECTURE AS AUTOBIOGRAPHY

Translated from the Italian by Thomas Muirhead

First published in the United Kingdom in 2005 by
Thames & Hudson Ltd, 181A High Holborn, London WC1V 7QX

www.thamesandhudson.com

First published in the United States of America in 2005 in paperback by
Thames & Hudson Inc., 500 Fifth Avenue, New York, New York 10110

thamesandhudsonusa.com

© 2005 IdeArte srl, Milano

British Library Cataloguing-in-Publication Data
A catalogue record for this book is available from the British Library

Library of Congress Catalog Card Number 2005904460

ISBN-13: 978-0-500-28583-1
ISBN-10: 0-500-28583-7

Printed and bound in Italy

CONTENTS

Every work of art reveals its creator; an exact image and likeness of the person who made it…
– Carlo Mollino, *Il linguaggio dell'architettura*, 1949

PREFACE

It was only at his death in 1973, when his friend Bruno Zevi [6] wrote a moving obituary for *L'Espresso*, that Carlo Mollino was finally given proper recognition by the architectural establishment. In 1982, it was Zevi again who organized the first large general retrospective exhibition on Mollino, at the Fiera di Bari, which was curated by the present author and excellently designed by Silvio Coppola. In 1986, in *L'Espresso*, Zevi reviewed the first edition of this book. More recently, again in *L'Espresso*, he fought, with characteristic passion, to save Mollino's Lago Nero cableway station and ski-lodge, built in 1947 and the only masterpiece by this great architect to have survived irreversible alteration or total destruction – even though by that stage the building was in a very badly deteriorated condition.

Breaking his own rule of not writing introductions for books, Zevi agreed to write one for this second edition of my act of homage to Mollino, but sadly in the meantime he died unexpectedly. To keep his promise alive, however, I am beginning this new edition with a slightly unorthodox 'collage' of some articles and writings by Zevi, and one or two others which will give the reader a useful overview of Mollino's life and work.

The first piece takes the form of an amusing character portrait of Mollino at the very beginning of his career [3]. It describes him – or at least pretends to describe him – as he was on the day he received his degree in architecture from the Polytechnic of Turin. Almost presciently, this affectionately written caricature captures the spirit of his whole life. It was written and published by some of his fellow-students in 1931, in a spirit that falls somewhere between *goliardismo* (a kind of scholastic lampooning common in Italy during the Fascist period) and the provocative spirit of Futurism.

The other three pieces, all by Zevi, can be read as an impassioned overview of Mollino's entire output. *En passant*, Zevi incorporates two important testimonials by Giuseppe Pagano and Roberto Gabetti. Taken together, these accounts serve to show how it was simply by always remaining exactly who he was that Mollino found himself cast as the *enfant terrible* of Italian architecture. Other assessments made since then, whether praising or damning, do not substantially diverge from that interpretation.

– *Giovanni Brino, December 2004*

'Carlo Mollino? A man surely in league with the Devil. When he opens his mouth and speaks, out come Gillette blades, razors, scimitars, and splinters of glass, but also enchanted gardens and monstrous flowers in colours nobody has ever seen. He claims to be a native of Turin, but we know he is a Saracen to the core. His existence is a combination of lethargic incubation and then ferocious, unstoppable action. When he is not making mayhem, he dozes in a sordid torpor, perhaps for months, with only short breaks for eating. And when he awakes, he is a pitiful picture of the most pathetic imbecility. But suddenly, never in doubt as to what his basic intentions are, he embarks on some wild adventure and goes through with it to the end, without a moment's hesitation.

He has a way of getting absolutely whatever he wants, at any cost: there can be no doubt that he is a diabolical character. In architecture, he claims to be one of the so-called 'Purists' and professes an aesthetic of magic equilibriums and poignant relationships. Once he said to us 'a client dies, but the work of architecture remains, remains down the ages'. This makes us fear he may have to spend his life murdering his clients.

Some people say that when he becomes an architect he will become as rich as a buccaneer; but we would not be surprised either if he ended up doing stunts in some equestrian circus, or performing acrobatics on the high bar and the flying trapeze.

In the summer he simply disappears. He wanders off around Europe, or sometimes hides himself away in the solitude of the Alps, where, in the most princely of surroundings, he basks in the embraces of a private collection of marvellous lovers, gathered from who knows where'.

– 'We, who are about to take our degrees': 'The Architects' Wake', 8 April, Year IX of the Fascist Era, Turin, 1931

2. 'The Aerial Deception'. Photograph of Carlo Mollino the aviator, taken by Piero Martina against the background of a blown-up aerial photograph of Manhattan, 1942

3. Caricature by Michele Guerrisi of Carlo Mollino on the day of his university degree award ceremony, 1931

3

BRUNO ZEVI THE DEATH OF MOLLINO

4. Portrait of Mollino
in Casa Miller, *c.* 1938

'In 1941, when presenting the new building for the Turin Ippica, Giuseppe Pagano made an analysis of Carlo Mollino's approach to architecture that would hold true over and over again, even in late projects like the Teatro Regio or Palazzo Affari. He wrote: "So intense, so acute is the spatial exaltation in Mollino's sensibility, so natural, so admirably totalitarian his need to break with every dogma of vile classicism, so overpowering his desire to avoid every indulgence, welding a whole composition into a single coherent vision, so complete in each part and permanently resolved, that he really does succeed in pushing the decomposition of space to its final limit, creating a poetic of the functional which denies all the values of a formal conventionalism. He then recomposes space into new, unquiet relationships, saturated with strange and expressive internal tensions, like those of an animate being, living independently of the architect's will, or as a scenographic pretext consisting only of lights and shadows, without any definitive physical solidity. This magical, atmospheric state is the most accentuated characteristic of Mollino's personality. It is given to him, above all, by his will to dominate space, to move it, to break every state of quietude so as to suggest new physiognomies. It seems that he is able to make volumes compress and expand, that he has the capacity to provoke illusory perspectives that multiply themselves fluidly. And yet, if we observe these forms calmly and ask why they are as they are, thinking about them in the light of the coldest functionality, we have to recognize that nothing about them is arbitrary; no accusations of capricious decorative transposition can be moved against this architect. His work is not – as some of his curvilinear predilections might lead some to think – the posthumous reappearance of a floral stylism we have left behind. It is a firm domination of the inventive spirit, and an almost musical exaltation of space, which he expresses in outpourings that are filled with spontaneous emotive force."

Mollino never bothered to reply to those questions so delicately raised by the enthusiastic, but clearly disconcerted, Pagano. Pagano continued: "In this game, conducted by its extremely cunning director, do we not see something of a weakness for purely painterly images that cannot be built, an intellectual's research into abstract layouts? To put it better, do we not see a sentimental surrender to the surrealism of a world that remains suspended, perhaps a hypothesis he has not yet formulated, or even a search for some interior, personal, absurd, poetic space? Certainly there is a complex play of mysterious dissociative forces at work in Mollino, and they are pushing him into some very risky areas. But paradoxically, some rebellious longing he has for the poetic seems to keeps him safely away from all utilitarian vulgarities and every monumental rhetoric. Getting himself into an almost uncontrollable state of excitement, he actually tastes the physicality of architectural space, and finds his model in it, as a holy madman would. He seems to possess an unconscious and stubborn resistance, as he goes very close to errors of judgment without ever falling over the edge. This is the best testimony I can give to his intelligence and good taste."

Even as a sixty-eight-year old, Mollino was still the same. An incorrigible *enfant terrible*, with a character so abrasive that it was sometimes impossible even to speak to him, he would shut himself away in Via Pamparato, in his father's nineteenth-century office, where he would profane its noble, thoughtful surroundings with deeply disturbed drawings and blasphemous photographs. Then, to discharge his incredible accumulated energy, he would fling himself into death-defying exploits as stunt pilot, champion skier, or the inebriated driver of racing cars. He diced with death, fed himself on emotions, and transmuted his sexual ardour into architectural images of plastic sinuousnesses, spaces without end, in an anomalous language of his own that was caught between the rational and the organic, extremely solid but also curvilinear, elegant, and very ambiguous; like Le Corbusier as seen by a man filled with the spirit of Guarino Guarini. But accusations of being neo-baroque made him livid; his freedom from Cubistic geometricism came from somewhere else, and followed the evolution of racing cars and aeroplane design as, devoid of every angularism, he completely bypassed that architecture of the square box and the repetitive space-containers that look as if they have came off some production line.

As a professor at the Faculty of Architecture at the Polytechnic of Turin, his teaching was known to be discontinuous and attracted much criticism; but he was also one of a very few teachers who were capable of determining a cultural direction for architecture. And if in Turin now there are perhaps ten or twenty young architects of real quality, in significant measure this is thanks to Mollino. He focused on architecture as a *métier* and an art, instead of dressing up in the clothes of an amateur sociologist; and he detested the paternalism of those who brought their personal existential crises into the school.

Among the numerous buildings he completed, the Lago Nero cableway station and ski-lodge, near Sestrière, in the Alps, stands out: a timber building on a stone base, it explodes in the landscape with an undulating reinforced concrete terrace that powerfully overhangs in space, and is protected

5

5. Mezzanine landing with 'window beam' above the riding school at the 'Ippica' (Turin Equestrian Club). Photograph by Carlo Mollino, 1941

from the weather by a windshield of tempered glass. G. E. Kidder Smith judged this building "one of the most three-dimensional works of modern Italian architecture. Not only is it difficult to view head-on, its volumetric arrangement requires us to move around it as if it were a sculpture. This anti-Renaissance attitude is particularly comforting in a country where there is too much façadism."

Mollino himself was more fond of Casa Garelli, in the Val d'Ayas, which he completed in 1965. This consisted of the dismantled parts of a traditional chalet, the Taleuc "rascard", which he rebuilt on a different site on the outskirts of Champoluc: the pieces were the same, including the characteristic mushroom supports with stone heads, but a few of his personalizing touches were enough to make the building emanate a completely new message.

He also adopted a similar approach in more demanding works, beginning with the Teatro Regio. "Finding oneself surrounded by Renaissance and Baroque presences", he said, "it is better to seem to be in agreement, in a dignified way, and to use polite arguments without pushing and shoving, so as not be excluded from the scene." The result? He infuriated everyone, the nostalgics and the ultra-moderns, because his building did not follow any fashion of one or the other kind. And the Mollino "problem" is still there, impenetrable beyond every classification, requiring long consideration. Even his sudden death came as a shock: not in an aeroplane or skiing as we all expected, but quietly, without any fuss, in the desert of his atelier.'

— Bruno Zevi, 'La scomparsa di Carlo Mollino. L'antiaccademico a trecento all'ora' ['The death of Carlo Mollino. The anti-academic at three-hundred miles an hour'], in L'Espresso, 9 September 1973

BRUNO ZEVI IT IS RIGHT TO REBEL

6

6. Bruno Zevi with Carlo Levi, 1956

'"Writing about Mollino is not an easy thing to do", warned Roberto Gabetti…"In fact, for more than a decade since his death, the complexity of deciphering his personality has prevented us from looking at it again, while the critical reticence surrounding him has been almost palpably hostile."

One of the most genial and enigmatic exponents of the avant-garde, "unconventional at all costs, pushed to an incredible extreme of individualism", Mollino belongs to that tradition of the solitary inventor which stretches from Leonardo da Vinci to Buckminster Fuller. Along with his output of buildings, furniture, stage sets, design objects, inventions, and urban plans, he accumulated an impressive series of patents for reinforced concrete beehive structures or movable joints and junctions, cigar lighters, and aerodynamic car-body designs like the Bisiluro racing car, in which he won the prestigious Le Mans trophy.

Born in 1905 in Turin, his formative years coincided with the wild period of "Second Futurism". But he resisted all possibilities of allying himself with any individual or group. Without ever admitting to Futurist tendencies, he had inherited to the full Marinetti's taste for speed, and his constant reference was to the world of machines. As for Le Corbusier, the only cultural impetus he can be said to have taken from him was a sensitivity to the logic of industrial production. But this was stoked by an organicism, and integrated with "a pleasure in double meanings, an ambiguity". An exceptionally gifted artisan, he elaborated designs that were "inconvenient and sensational", and came from his other lives as stunt pilot, downhill skier, racing-car driver, photographer, fashion designer, erotomaniac, traveller, and worshipper of the occult.

Brino describes Mollino's career in five phases: his youthful experiments, culminating in the masterpiece of the Turin Ippica building of 1937; then the enforced repose caused by the war, when he worked on interior designs and studied ways of living; the postwar period, characterized by the Lago Nero cableway station and ski-lodge, and other mountain buildings, from his "marine interiors" to splendid rearrangements of private residences; then his refuge in motor racing and flying, after the death of his father in 1953 – interrupted only by the project for a ballroom and the competition for Palazzo del Lavoro – and then his work after 1964, with completion of the Chamber of Commerce and the Teatro Regio.

He was inspired on the one hand by the vernacular and, on the other, by an overwhelmingly baroque sense of space, made mobile by a plastic fury, that "rebellious need for poetry" that Pagano identified in 1941, trying to describe his abnormal behaviour. Mollino's relationship with Turin was in fact characterized by "an absolute lack of interest, and even an attitude of scorn".

In 1960, the municipal administration of Turin approved demolition of the Ippica. The cableway station and ski-lodge building at Lago Nero was abandoned to vandals and bad weather. The Chamber of Commerce and the Regio "were attacked with an obsessiveness that went far beyond normal criticism".

Mollino, "the magician of talent", was a heretic equipped with a creative courage that is intolerable for all conservatives'.

– Bruno Zevi, 'Ribellarsi è giusto', L'Espresso, 9 February 1986

BRUNO ZEVI SAVE THE CHALET

'Italy neglects her few masterpieces of modern architecture: Luigi Moretti's Fencing Hall in Rome; Carlo Scarpa's Olivetti shop in Venice and, at 2,400 metres above sea level in Sauze d'Oulx, Carlo Mollino's station and hotel, in the locality of Lago Nero. This project was left almost completed in 1947, after continual modifications dictated by the genius of its Author. Its aerobatic external stair, its chimney, its wooden gutters, all lunge forward in an indulgence of curves and overhangs: "We must make this building fly", he said. The building is Surrealist, Futurist, and Organicist, rich in inventions, in the baroque manner. It was abandoned after 1958 and has become reduced to an incredible state of destruction. It desperately needs to be restored, now. We have already lost Mollino's building for the Turin Ippica. We cannot allow ourselves another such waste.'

– Bruno Zevi, 'Salvate la baita', L'Espresso, 3 June 1999

'Dear Zevi,

At last I can give you some wonderful news we have been awaiting for years: the chalet is saved!

Thanks to financing from the Municipality of Sauze d'Oulx and the Regional Government (via the Community of the Mountains) and with a blitz of only three months (August through October), and the collaboration of an enthusiastic firm of contractors it has been possible to carry out the first Lot of recovery work, worth about 400 million lire.... Our restoration work, now completed, includes most of the major features of the chalet (the "baita", as you call it).... We still need to restore the 'Terranova' external plaster, and all of the interiors, which will be used as a restaurant and bar. The roof space, as before, will be used for sleeping accommodation. The lower floor in reinforced concrete will contain Italy's first Museum of the History of Skiing; this is a use that will certainly be in tune with the building, and which would have pleased Mollino, who was a skier himself, and a great connoisseur of mountain architecture....

To celebrate the recovery of the building, the Editor of Idea Books [the original publishers] would like to republish my book Carlo Mollino: Architecture as Autobiography, which you originally reviewed in L'Espresso and is now out of print.... I would like to ask you now if you would be kind enough to write the introduction. I would like to thank you in advance for this, and for anything else you can still do to help the "baita". Please do not hesitate to contact me for any further information you require. With best wishes,'

– Fax from Giovanni Brino to Bruno Zevi, 13 October 1999

'Dear Brino,

Your letter has made me happy. Well done to yourself and Rajneri. You've saved a masterpiece. You have paid best possible homage to my friend Mollino. Bravissimi! My enthusiastic applause.

As for the presentation, or introduction, for your rewritten book, I always turn down this kind of invitation. I don't believe in introductions, so I don't write them.

But is Mollino an exception? Certainly. And if you can't find anyone else to write the presentation, I'll do it.

Cordially,

Bruno Zevi'

– Fax from Bruno Zevi to Giovanni Brino, 14 October 1999

7. The Lago Nero sled-pull station. Photograph by Berkialla-Bressano, 1948

8. Fax from Bruno Zevi to Giovanni Brino